HOW TO MAKE MONEY ONLINE
Strategies to Earn Passive Income and Impact Audiences with Your Wisdom

GRACE JONAS

Dedication

Dedicated to Clara Jones.

Copyright

No part of this book is allowed to be reproduced in any form without approval from the author.

Table of Content

CHAPTER ONE

Finding the Right Niche

In the vast and crowded world of online content creation, discovering and developing your specific niche is absolutely essential for standout success. Rather than randomly creating according to your passing interests, take the time upfront to strategically research, analyze, and reflect upon where you can provide the most value based on your innate strengths, knowledge, and passion points.

Start by brainstorming a list of your interests, skills, experiences, education, training, hobbies, and more. Look for intersections and common themes that feel aligned to who you uniquely are. Notice areas where you have deep knowledge or convey infectious enthusiasm when discussing the topic. The goal is to find "your people" - those you can serve, understand, and impact the most powerfully because you inherently "get" them.

Conduct keyword research using tools like Google Keyword Planner to assess search volume and competition on niche ideas you are exploring. While you don't have to dominate the most competitive keywords, make sure there is enough search demand from prospective followers genuinely interested in consuming content in your niche. After all, without an audience actually seeking your type of content, there will be few people to ultimately monetize.

Reflect honestly on your appetite for creating regular, ongoing content in specific niches over the long haul. The niche(s) you select will become the foundational beat you cover potentially for years to come through blogs, videos, podcasts, and more. So you must remain excited to discuss the intricacies of the topic nearly every day. If you grow bored easily covering a niche, it shows through lackluster content...and disengaged audiences.

Consider expanding into multiple profitable niches over time under the umbrella of an overarching brand centered around your core expertise. Gary

Vaynerchuk transitioned from a pure wine focus to also cover social media marketing, NFTs, entrepreneurship, investment advice and more. He did so gradually while retaining his high energy style that had attracted his original following with Wine Library TV.

Become a Recognized Expert

With niche clarity in place, pour your heart and soul into truly mastering every aspect of the domain. Immerse yourself in the deepest intricacies of the field so you can share hard-earned wisdom and experience, not just surface-level information easily found elsewhere. Read extensively, reach out to top creators and pick their brain, take associated courses, and put what you learn into practice. Soon you will discover meaningful insights and creative angles on the niche that inspire your own educational content aimed at helping others.

The authority and influence you build has direct correlation to the value you provide for others in your niche. So focus first and foremost on serving your audience rather than what you personally will gain through fame and fortune. Show genuine care for their struggles in the niche and apply your expertise to deliver solutions in a spirit of service. When your audience recognizes this authentic desire to impact their lives, they will reward you with engagement and loyalty over the long-term.

Patience is key, as expertise is rarely built overnight...but rather the result of years spent relentlessly honing your skills and knowledge around a niche. Early on, it's natural to feel like an imposter speaking on topics with far more seasoned voices already out there. Push past this by consistently showing up authentically as you share your evolving niche journey. Given enough time and consistency, you will wake up one day a respected expert worthy of monetizing the audience that has come to rely on your specialized wisdom.

Create Written Content: Blogs, Articles, Newsletters

The Power of the Written Word

In an online world filled with flashy videos and clever memes, the power of old-school written content remains as relevant as ever. Well-crafted blogs, articles, and newsletters continue capturing audience mindshare while also converting readers into buyers. Leverage the versatility and cost-efficiency of writing to build awareness and income streams through platforms like email, social media, and your own sites.

Blogs remain a stalwart for establishing niche authority and showcasing expertise around focused topics. Commit to consistently publishing longer-form posts weekly or monthly to drive organic traffic and demonstrate your capabilities. Enrich blog content with relevant statistics, actionable advice, personal anecdotes, response to current events, answers to common questions, product reviews, local news, and more.

Repurpose blog content into articles for added exposure, tailoring length and style for the intended outlet such as industry publications, local newspapers, or high-traffic websites accepting contributor submissions. Become a reliable expert column writer covering your niche while benefiting from the built-in visibility of the hosting site.

For even wider distribution, adapt articles into snippets for social media posting, especially on platforms like LinkedIn where business decision-makers concentrate. Pin eye-catching excerpts natively to Pinterest boards saving relevant images. Tweet compelling statistics, advice or questions to spark conversation. Upload list posts and tip articles tailored for the vertical scrolling experience on Facebook and Instagram.

Newsletters continue to excel as personalized, subscriber-only destinations where you're most engaged community members gather for exclusives they won't find anywhere else. Reserve in-depth guides, special discounts, giveaways, first looks at new products/services, and early-bird event access for email subscribers only. This incentivizes newsletter sign-ups and retains loyal readers.

Make Mobile Browsing a Priority

With over 60% of website traffic now originating on mobile devices, responsive web design is mandatory when publishing written content online. If viewers struggle to read or navigate your website or blogs on their phones, they will instantly move elsewhere...taking potential pageviews with them.

Enable pinch/zoom functionality so text can be easily expanded for mobile reading. Use minimal vertical space on pages to reduce excess scrolling on small screens. Include quality captioning on images and graphics for visually impaired viewers. Allow easily tapping phone numbers to dial directly on smartphones. Embed calls-to-action so mobile viewers convert directly without device switching.

Writing for Impact and Income

While passion fuels your content creation rather than pursuit of money alone, intellectual property deserves being valued and compensated accordingly. Reframe writing from an expense into income center through memberships, tip jars, value-driven ecommerce, and more.

Gate some written content behind paid memberships at varied access levels with perks like ad-free reading experiences and unlockable archives of past content. Brainstorm relevant products tied to your niche that readers may find valuable for purchase based on the expertise shared through your writing. Collaborate with brands serving your audience to unlock sponsorship and affiliate sales income.

The written word remains as relevant as ever in our increasingly distracted digital age. Cut through fleeting videos and saturated social streams by delivering concentrated value focused on serving niche needs. Consistent high quality writing ranked by search engines continues capturing reader mindshare. Monetize and sustain your efforts directly from those benefiting most from your carefully chosen words.

Produce Videos, Podcasts, and Images

Here is an overview of producing videos, podcasts, and images to grow your online audience and income:

Videos

Video content helps showcase your personality while communicating complex topics visually. Invest in basic video equipment like a quality webcam/camera, microphone, and simple editing software. Set up an informal home studio or record videos outdoors showcasing relevant settings. Boost production value overtime as income allows to keep early videos simple and launch faster.

Outline tight scripts hitting key talking points to keep videos focused yet conversational. Weave in personal stories and examples viewers relate to on an emotional level. Tease future videos to encourage binge viewing while building video libraries around niche topics for easy discoverability later.

Podcasts

Podcasting aligns perfectly with lengthy commutes and routine tasks needing accompaniment. As listeners feel they personally know hosts visiting their headphones, build strong connection through candid personal stories in addition to expert interviews and focused topic discussions.

Rather than expensive equipment and editing, concentrate first on value-driven conversations. Record interviews over video chat platforms before upgrading to fancier microphone set ups. Boost audio quality in post production to keep earliest episodes simple and launch faster.

Promote episodes through platforms like Instagram and LinkedIn extracting insight quotes as images/snippets driving back to full audio. Over time, trim longer recordings into shorter segments increasing shareability and overall listenership.

Images

Capitalize on our strongly visual world by liberally incorporating niche relevant photos, graphics, illustrations and more to catch reader attention while breaking up blocks of text.

Curate free images from aggregators like Pexels and Pixabay for starter content while building original collections over time. Contract visual creators on platforms like Fiverr to produce custom images promoting your brand and style.

License your own photographs, designs, logos and more through passive income marketplaces like Getty Images and Creative Market. Images require some upfront time to create but continue earning royalties indefinitely.

The combination of video, audio and images woven alongside quality writing engages audiences across preferred media preferences while showcasing your niche expertise from multiple angles.

Connect With Your Audience on Social Media

Choosing Platforms Strategically

Rather than spreading yourself thin across every social media platform, thoughtfully select ones aligning closest to your niche, personality and content formats. While Facebook continues dominating overall with its broad demographic appeal, niche sites like LinkedIn and Pinterest concentrate valuable audiences.

Consider crossover potential between your specialization and various platforms' strengths when deciding where to focus. For example, visually dynamic content suited for Pinterest's scrapbook-style feeds might struggle gaining traction on the discussion-centric Facebook. Podcasters drive more engagement distributing audio snippets natively on Spotify over text-focused platforms.

Get Personal and Authentic

Social media creates space for community far beyond impersonal broadcasting. Share your authentic self, quirky personality and deeper passions to resonate emotionally with followers craving genuine connection. Spark two-way conversations through interactive polls, AMAs (Ask Me Anything), reactions to current events and niche related Q&As.

While privacy remains important, consider going live or posting Stories more informally from personal contexts beyond your desk. Give fans a peek behind the curtain into your home, family, hobbies and even failures. This level of vulnerability breeds loyalty not garnered from overly professional, polished personas alone.

Consistent Engagement Wins

Rather than periodic promotional blasting of new offerings, integrate consistent value-focused engagement into your regular routine. Carve out small daily/weekly time for social listening and interactions.

Like and thoughtfully reply to follower comments, even if just a few daily. Share user generated content displaying your products/services in real-world contexts. Reshare credible niche articles from leaders in your field.

Monitor notifications, read DMs, identify emergent conversations to join, new influencers to potentially collaborate with and adjust strategies according to real-time feedback.

Listen First, Sell Second

Resist overly pitching products or services without first understanding individual needs and build caring relationships, even at scale. Survey followers to discover demographics, desires and pain points so you can tailor content accordingly. Poll for feedback on new offerings before investing heavily in development.

Rather than just routing followers to buy things, craft tailored recommendations based on listening. Guide them gently through the discovery process until organically ready to purchase rather than high pressure sales tactics.

True influence sparks when audiences recognize your concern for their growth ahead of simply increasing transactions. Sincere engagement mixed with value focused content over time convert followers into loyal brand champions.

Social media facilitates intimate community beyond physical constraints when leveraged for transparency, accountability and nurturing relationships through regular interactions. Prioritize cultivating emotional bonds with niche followers over mass reach across disconnected demographics. The quality of digital relationships eclipse chasing vanity metrics alone.

Maximize quality and consistency to grow viewership

Obsess Over Production Quality

In a sea of free online content flooding every niche, production quality becomes a key differentiator setting your work apart. While lacking Hollywood-sized budgets, apply creativity toward enhancing legitimacy. Write tight scripts or outlines to communicate ideas clearly. Edit videos maintaining crisp pacing without rambling. Invest in intro/outro music underscoring brand personality. Capture engaging thumbnails and graphics spread across social media. Prioritize finally conveying value over fancy equipment alone. Boost legitimacy over time by reinvesting revenue directly into better gear improving future quality.

Consistency Creates Trust

Unlike sporadic viral moments, meaningful loyalty develops through predictable consistency allowing audiences to rely on you. Establish cadence early whether daily vlogs, weekly podcasts or monthly newsletters so followers know what to expect. Maintaining reliable programming requires discipline resisting distraction by life's unavoidable ups and downs. During periods lacking creative inspiration, modify formats minimizing production time without comprising consistency. Bank pre-recorded episodes or replay evergreen content rather than leave programming holes losing subscriber momentum. Software automations help maintain steady social posting amidst busyness. Consistency earns authority by demonstrating lifelong dedication to nurturing niche community versus chasing temporary fads.

Obsess Over Optimizing Discovery

Quality content alone means little if failing to connect with those needing your message most. Audit your niche by regularly assessing top search terms and monitoring trending topics. Identify seasonal spikes in demand to align programming with audience seeking your expertise at yearly peaks. Refresh old evergreen content tying into emergent searcher demand. Share content natively on platforms where niche followers already gather, commenting to spark algorithm-friendly engagement. Follow hashtags where your people congregate for real-time trend spotting. Strategically guest post on reputable niche sites expanding reach to similar audiences. Request podcast interviews on top shows reaching your target demographic. initial small numbers reflect focused targeting over mass general appeal. Optimize self-produced content for search and social sharing allowing value to spread organically over time by empowering advocates.

Analyze and Respond

Rather than guesswork, leverage free analytics from website CMS, email providers, and built-in social media insight tools showing real-time traction. Review traffic sources, top pages, conversions, and engagement rates. Use A/B testing to experiment with imagery, headlines, captions, and calls to action to optimize impact. Poll your audience for suggestions on desired topics and improve programming accordingly. Analytics reveal who truly connects with your work, empowering better resource allocation to double down on what works based on data instead of ego.

Become a Resource Hub

Maximize loyalty by becoming a trusted one-stop resource hub versus creating isolated content. Develop comprehensive learning academies with modules tackling niche topics from varied angles. Curate exhaustive lists of top tools both free and paid serving audience needs. Publish multi-part guides diving deep versus brief surface posts. Facilitate community spaces for discussion and amplification around challenges they face. Recognize emerging leaders contributing their own expertise in collaborations elevating the entire ecosystem. Expand authority by spotlighting those already respected alongside your own voice. Welcome diverse perspectives even when differing from yours. Position your channels as a rich environment for audience growth more than platform for self-promotion alone. By generously providing endless value, you organically earn viewership and income over the long-term.

CHAPTER TWO

Monetize Your Content and Knowledge

Display ads and affiliate marketing

Display advertising places highly targeted promotional messages alongside content consumed by niche site visitors. Unlike interrupting viewers with disruptive video commercials, display ads blend organically into page designs when executed effectively.

Start by placing native ads on industry forums and niche interest blogs aligning with your target customer demographic. Select sites with engaged, actively commenting communities and lower advertising costs per impression. This stretches limited ad budgets further thanks to hyper focused targeting.

Experiment with size variations from single post sidebar widgets to header banner placements. Monitor click-through-rates (CTR) and conversion performance for each ad unit, tweaking creative and placement on underperformers. Continually test new sites and ad formats using small initial budgets before scaling winners.

Eventually graduate into paid social promotions and display network placements based on interest and search behavior. For example, advertise ecommerce products to those reading related articles or already following niche influencers. Show service ads only to followers of complementary brands. Facebook, Instagram and Pinterest's detailed audience segmentation takes guessing work out of targeted ad alignment.

Affiliate Marketing Allies

Affiliate marketing enlists others to promote your products/services in exchange for commission on resulting sales. Also known as cost-per-acquisition (CPA) programs, affiliates earn predetermined bonuses for each customer converted. This pay-for-performance model limits promotional risk while incentivizing networks to relentless drive conversions.

Attract affiliates by offering competitive commissions relative to perceived value of your offerings. Make signup seamless by integrating robust partner portals where creators easily access promotional assets like ads, product imagery and discount codes tied to their unique referral links.

Build relationships with influencers, bloggers and information product creators serving your customer demographic. Encourage organic integration of your offerings instead of overt endorsements. For example fitness bloggers may highlight your new workout guide within thoughtful recommendations of their "favorite resources for getting in shape."

Continually test commission structures with higher payouts for influencers driving increased unit volumes. Tier programs to increase commissions after affiliates reach incremental conversion milestones.

Display ads and affiliate partnerships expand promotional reach when resources limit doing everything solely in-house. Just be sure to accurately track attribution, so you pay only directly for successful conversions generated by partners. This limits risk while allowing scaled growth impossible alone.

Sell Information Products Like Ebooks

Become the Author of Your Niche

Publishing an eBook establishes your niche authority while creating new profit center. Rather than giving away all expertise for free, package high-value content into longer-form guides people happily purchase.

Start by outlining chapters around questions frequently received from your audience base. Deliver more nuanced training than possible in a blog post or video. Build a compelling resource hub enticing readers to go deeper across interconnected facets of your specialty.

Repurpose the best existing articles and webinars to expedite initial eBook creation. Then enhance reused content transforming it into new formats and angles tailored specifically for the book. Interview niche leaders or profile existing customers as case studies for added engagement.

Pricing Psychology

When valuing expertise into buyable assets, consider perceived worth over production costs alone. Price too low and audiences might dismiss quality. Price too high could limit accessibility for those needing solutions most.

Test customer response at increasing price points between $7 and $27 before committing long-term. Some niches sustain premium value better than others. For example financial analysts or executive coaches reasonably command rates beyond lifestyle bloggers or musicians.

Frame spending as an investment into solving struggles or learning high-income skills. Compare eBook prices to a single specialty coffee rather than big-ticket purchases requiring larger financial consideration. This mental positioning eases consumer buying friction.

Smooth Checkout Wins Sales

Emphasize speed and convenience ensuring readers convert downloads directly when ready rather than adding extra sign-in walls. Require only essential buyer fields like name and email resisting optional info only valuable for marketing purposes. Offer instant delivery of electronic products directly upon payment finalization so customers access content immediately reducing fear of abandonment.

Welcome various payment forms including internationally friendly options like PayPal. Consider installment plans breaking costs into smaller recurring credit card charges over multiple months for expensive high-value items. Test bundled discounts packaging your eBook with other complementary courses or services.

Promote Sustainably

Resist heavy promotion of your eBook alone or audiences feel continually pitched for financial self-interest over their growth. Instead highlight the guide only a few times during launch month alongside regular educational content before returning focus back to free material. This balances monetization with consistent value buildup reinforcing your expertise.

Sustain sales through occasional "secret" discounts to email subscribers, affiliate partnerships with those selling into similar niches and bonuses for bundling various info products together over time.

Information eBooks establish your niche capabilities while earning income directly from those benefiting most from your carefully packaged wisdom. Just remember value-focused motives serve long-term prosperity over quick cash alone.

Launch Courses, Coaching Programs, Consultations

Here is a 897-word engaging elaboration on launching online courses, coaching programs, and consultations:

Empowering Transformation Through Ongoing Training

Beyond static information products like books and pdf guides, invite niche audiences into transformative learning journeys through multimedia online courses, high-touch coaching programs, and personalized consulting sessions leveraging your hard-earned expertise around the clock.

Online Courses: Your Always-On Professor

With detailed video lessons organized into modules, online courses simulate the experience of attending a top university led by you as friendly professor of your niche. Bring dry concepts alive on-screen through sketches, relevant images, simple animations, on-location demonstrations, interviews with industry leaders, supplemental pdf downloads and more. Package together 8-12 core video lessons users access on-demand adding interactivity through self-check comprehension quizzes, community discussion forums, and optional advanced training modules available for additional purchase.

Welcome new students with a warm video intro outlining the learning journey complete with roadmap of key topics covered and milestones achieved upon completion. Foster ongoing engagement through live virtual office hours allowing for real-time Q&A, polls soliciting feedback to improve future lessons, exclusive discounts on complementary tools/services, early access to new courses under development, and certificates of completion elevating professional legitimacy. Send reminder emails when new modules release and share student success stories cultivating community. Online courses provide reliable revenue through high margin passive income stream as new enrollees join every week without ongoing time investment after initial creation.

Coaching   Programs: Ongoing   Expert Partnership

For those seeking more individualized support applying training concepts directly to business or life goals, launch a limited enrollment high touch group coaching program. Provide application forms or discovery calls to intentionally select committed participants aligned to your expertise and coaching methodology. Outline specific ambitious outcomes possible within a defined multi-month engagement including key performance indicators to benchmark starting abilities against growth by end. Lead monthly training calls where members receive direct expertise while bonding through discussions outlining action items completed, challenges faced, breakthrough insights earned and goals reached since previous session. Assign support buddies for increased accountability between calls. Schedule one-on-one support sessions as needed to provide personalized guidance for unique situations. Conduct pre/post assessments quantifying progress gained across both hard and soft skills developed. Celebrate successful completion through highlighting their achievements to your wider audience. You can even enroll top students as future coaches expanding your ability to facilitate impact. Although limited in number per cohort, coaching programs deliver premium pricing packages and extremely satisfied brand advocates upon completion.

Consulting: Dedicated Expert Problem Solving

For those overwhelmed tackling ambitious projects solo or organizations/businesses seeking outside expertise supporting strategic direction, offer personalized consulting packages tailored to clearly defined needs and budgets. Start with clarity calls identifying scope of desired outcomes, key milestones, required assets and optimal timeline given constraints. Next quote pricing packages aligned to complexity, seniority level working on deliverables, whether one-time or ongoing advisory over multiple months etc. Ask strategic questions highlighting risks/opportunities frequently missed by clients tackling similar projects in isolation absent insider perspective only your expertise provides. Invest time required delivering audits, plans, designs, spreadsheets, executed campaigns, staff training programs and anything else outlined within project specifications. Check in consistently with updates, overcoming unexpected hurdles proactively through open communication channels. Review results in depth against original benchmarks and goals outlined determining successes to highlight in future sales conversations with similar prospective clients. Provide additional recommendations for long-term sustainability. Consulting services provide premium income streams while making broad impact across entire organizations or industries.

By leveraging your hard-earned knowledge across customized ongoing learning experiences, each student, coaching client or consulting customer magnifies expertise into previously impossible results now made achievable through direct access to you as niche expert they trust. Dedicate your abilities toward empowering their transformation first and financial prosperity naturally follows.

Maximize Value While Focusing On Impact

Leading With Generosity

Rather than prioritizing rapid monetization above all else, patiently earn influence through generous value sharing over time first. Consistently create free educational content driven purely by a spirit of service not hooks into eventual sales pitches. When audiences recognize authentic care for their personal journey ahead of financial motives, they more readily trust expert advice and product recommendations later.

Start by giving away your absolute best content rather than saving top secrets only for paying customers. Overdeliver value in advance allowing prospects to experience real transformation for themselves initially at no cost. For example, a health coach might share better sleep tips or favorite go-to healthy recipes versus only selling general wellness ebooks upfront. This "freemium" layer builds authority and reciprocates value to align with eventual paid offerings.

Embrace a mindset focused on maximizing impact first trusting monetization naturally follows without needing to explicitly force or overpromote at every turn. Avoid overly sales-focused language across content and messaging that feels self-promotional. For example describe a course as an "empowering entrepreneurship journey" rather than leading taglines with the price and discount crossed out. This frames decision making around aspirational outcomes ahead of monetary exchange alone.

Pricing As Investment, Not Expense

When launching paid products and services, lead messaging with incredible value gained versus focusing too heavily on costs, features or return-on-investment alone. For example emphasize life-changing skills attained through a course or profound business breakthroughs possible through high-level consulting ahead of program structures. This encourages purchase decisions based on aspirational vision over justification math exercises alone.

Creatively bundle digital downloads, membership access and live experiences allowing customers self-determine their ideal pathway matched to personal budgets. This maximizes accessibility to your offerings across income levels while generating multiple income streams back to your business. Just ensure to overdeliver value regardless of price points so cost variations reflect consumption preferences rather than quality limitations between staggered tiers.

Make it Memorable

Rather than formulaic courses packed with generic templates, maximize memorable impact through unique experiential learning unmatched elsewhere. Facilitate live coaching and small group collaborations fostering genuine relationships beyond solo digital consumption. Feature inspiring guest interviews sharing personal wisdom. Set aside dedicated office hours for customized 1-on-1 guidance. Release new bonus training modules across time rewarding customer loyalty. Schedule exclusive live events, insider community discussions and behind-the-scenes content reinforcing premium program perceptions. The goal is crafting lifelong memories merging expertise with personal breakthroughs - this sparks referrals and repeat purchases over selling one-off products alone.

Maximize Alliances

Assemble top-tier collaborators across complimentary niches amplifying well-rounded impact together versus going solo. Align with brands serving similar demographics. Recruit affiliate partners incentivized by commission structures proven to reward their ongoing promotion. Seek credible media outlets providing exposure unmatched on your own. Unite these allies around shared missions advancing your niche further together then feasible individually. Value conscious collaboration over isolated competition thinking.

While financial sustainability is important, avoid overly focusing on monetization metrics alone. Ground business decisions in actually transforming lives first. Consistently maximize delivered value, exceeding expectations across all offerings and price points. By generously overdelivering ahead of extracting payments, you organically build fierce loyalty - and ultimately prosperous monetization naturally follows in due time.

CHAPTER THREE

Leverage Passive Income Streams

Sell stock images, designs, templates, code, and more

Beyond traditional products and services, innovative modern income streams stem from licensing creative work including stock photography, graphic design templates, website themes/plugins, instructional videos, 3D models, app frameworks and source code components.

Stock Media Marketplaces

Photographers earn ongoing royalties selling images on stock media platforms like Shutterstock, Getty Images and Adobe

Stock. Shoot high-quality niche photos then describe contents thoroughly so images surface in buyer searches. Categories like business concepts, technology innovations and lifestyle moments generally sell best aligned to commercial usage in advertisements, digital publications, merchandise and more. Utilize extended license options retaining copyrights for representation across agencies bringing expanded distribution. Images licensed years ago often resurge in new found relevancy as visual trends cycle.

Graphic designers craft editable templates sold on marketplaces like Creative Market, DesignCuts and Creative Fabrica, catering especially to entrepreneurs launching new brands on a budget. Offer page layouts, social media graphics, logos, icons, illustrations, fonts, and more visual assets independent creators integrate directly into projects. Bundle assets into full suites by theme for increased perceived value. Designers set base prices then receive commissions on each sale with sites handling secure transactions, delivery and customer support. New template market entrants gain visibility allying with influencers through lucrative affiliate promotions to their engaged visual-focused followers.

Technical Digital Goods

Code savvy entrepreneurs build websites, mobile apps and SaaS platforms then sell complete systems or customizable frameworks on platforms like CodeCanyon. Provide installation documentation lowering adoption friction attracting less technical buyers to modify for their own use. Developers wanting more control choose specific code scripts and plugins boosting functions like animations, slideshows, Contact forms, shopping carts and dynamic reporting dashboards.

Some programmers choose open source licenses allowing free usage in return for acknowledged credit or requirements to share derivative versions publicly. This helps spread adoption more quickly initially, especially for projects focused on social impact over profit. Once widely used, developers introduce paid tiers or premium feature additions.

3D modeling and architectural professionals showcase interactive renders on TurboSquid. Vehicle designers display photo-realistic automotive visualizations with customization options. Game developers sell playable character models, sci-fi weapons, realistic terrain landscapes and more immersive gaming assets.

Companies lacking adequate internal design bandwidth increasingly source media assets from independent marketplace creators for faster, affordable innovation. This lifts financial and operational constraints on resource-strapped organizations now able to punch above their weight through readily available world-class digital goods tightly aligned to current needs.

Leverage niche skills mastered over years into finally monetizable offerings. Attract an audience already actively searching for your flavors of specialized abilities. While income potential remains variable, focus first on serving buyer needs consistently with tech acumen few individuals possess. By solving problems better than competitors, financial prosperity follows the trail of satisfied customers inherently.

Rent Out Space, Equipment, Tools (Airbnb Model)

Here is an overview of renting out space, equipment, and tools using the Airbnb business model:

Leveraging Underutilized Assets

Take inventory of any unused or spare capacity around your home, land, garage, or storage areas for potential rental income streams. With the rise of peer-to-peer rental platforms like NeighborGoods, you can now lend out infrequently used items in exchange for reasonable rental fees.

Rent Out Extra Space

Those with extra bedrooms, guest houses, RV pads or even just a spare parking spot can list them on accommodation networks like Airbnb, VRBO and HipCamp. Set competitive nightly rates relative to amenity quality and location desirability. Build a robust hosting profile with plenty of photos, detailed description of offerings, exact directions/check-in procedures and house rules to set expectations. Respond quickly to all rental inquiries. Once booked, ensure exceptional hospitality securing those coveted 5-star reviews for increased visibility on site algorithms to future travelers. Consider blocking certain high-demand seasons or holidays if wanting to limit hosting commitments.

Tool and Equipment Rentals

Handy DIYers with a well-stocked garage can offset costs by renting out specialty gear locally on sites like Fat Llama and ToolMe. List things like pressure washers, ladders, carpet cleaners, poder tools, lawn mowers, trucks, trailers, party supplies and more. Outline exact condition, operating procedures and included accessories so renters know what to expect. Rates vary based on tool type, quality and typical rental duration. Develop trust through owner ratings and rule enforcement around damage. Some platforms provide insurance protections. Just like popular sharing services for lodging, cars and bicycles, peer-to-peer equipment rental platforms enable money-saving access to items only needed temporarily.

The convenience and trust of the sharing economy unlock wider market access to assets previously trapped within individual ownership. Augment income through smarter redistribution of your own excess capacity to where needed most. Minimal effort is required to post and manage listings while idle assets work on your behalf.

Earning Royalties from Creative Work

In today's digital world, there are more opportunities than ever for creative professionals to earn ongoing royalties from their work. Whether you are an author, musician, artist, app developer, or other creative worker, your content and creations have the potential to generate passive income streams long after the initial effort of making them. By understanding royalty structures and marketing yourself and your work effectively, you can set up multiple revenue sources that require little maintenance but provide rewards for years to come.

Books and Ebooks

Traditionally, book authors earn royalties on each sale of their published works. Standard royalty rates in the publishing industry range between 10-15% of the sales price for print books and 25-50% for ebooks. Even if you go the independent self-publishing route through platforms like Amazon Kindle Direct Publishing or Barnes & Noble Press, their distribution channels make it possible to reach a wide audience and collect substantial royalties on an ongoing basis with little or no upfront or production costs. Optimizing metadata, smart pricing strategies, blog tours, and other marketing efforts can gain your book visibility and increase sales over time.

Music Streaming and Downloads

The rise of music streaming through services like Spotify and Apple Music has revolutionized the potential for musicians and songwriters to earn steady royalty income. Stream counts quickly add up, and with over 423 million music subscribers worldwide as of 2022, the royalty potential is immense. Industry standard streaming royalties range from $0.003 to $0.005 per stream. While it takes significant numbers to produce high earnings, the cumulative effect of gaining followers can result in stable passive income over months and years. Even independent artists can distribute their music through platforms like CD Baby and Tunecore which place songs across the major streaming services.

Stock Media

Photographs, video clips, illustrations, audio files, templates, fonts, and other downloadable design assets also have great passive income potential through stock media sites. You retain ownership and distribution rights to your work while stock media companies like Shutterstock, Getty Images, and GraphicRiver market it to customers across the globe. They handle printing, licensing and delivery while paying you generous royalties on each sale often ranging from 20-60% of earnings. The more content you have available in stock media libraries, the higher your potential distribution and royalties.

Advertising and Affiliate Programs

If you have a website, blog, YouTube channel, or podcast with a niche audience, incorporating affiliate links and advertising programs is a prime way to earn royalties. You get paid commission when your viewers click through ads or affiliate links and make purchases or sign up for service subscriptions. The more niche-focused your content, the more targeted and high-converting your royalty earning potential. Likewise, mobile apps that incorporate in-app advertising through networks like Google Ad Mob can earn revenues through impressions and click-throughs in a very passive manner.

The creative possibilities for profiting from royalties are truly endless in today's digital landscape. Wherever attention and audiences can be captured are opportunities to monetize through passive royalty earnings. By publishing across multiple platforms, maximizing discoverability, and utilizing affiliate and ad networks strategically, it's entirely feasible to build diversified income streams that require little effort to maintain but deliver ongoing rewards for your creative projects and content.

Dropshipping and Print-On-Demand

Dropshipping and print-on-demand (POD) are two incredibly popular ways to make money online with relatively little initial investment or inventory risk. By tapping into immense online marketplaces like Amazon, Shopify, and Etsy and leveraging suppliers that handle product fulfillment, you can open up potentially lucrative opportunities without needing to manufacture or stock products on your own. Experimenting with dropshipping and POD is the perfect way for aspiring entrepreneurs to venture into ecommerce.

Evaluating Dropshipping Niches

The beauty of dropshipping is selling popular or specialty products you don't actually own or purchase yourself. Researching profitable niches is key, as you ideally want consistent demand without a glut of competing dropshippers. Pet products, kitchen gadgets, specialty hobby gear, and electronics accessories tend to be reliable sellers. Use tools like Google Trends, Keyword Planner, and niche sites like SaleHoo to assess demand and supplier reliability. Consider running test ads for potential products on Facebook to gauge interest before committing fully.

Setting Up Your Dropshipping Operation

Having a polished brand website is key for inspiring customer trust, and platforms like Shopify and WooCommerce make the process easy. Choose a supplier like Spocket that handles orders, shipping, and returns. Import products to your store, set reasonable markup pricing, and integrate a payment processor. Focus your webpage content, social media posts, and advertising on solving consumer needs. As orders come in, your supplier handles fulfillment while you collect profits.

POD Experiments with Amazon Merch and Teespring

Experimenting with print-on-demand requires no upfront investment or inventory either and can capitalize on viral trends and enthusiastic fan bases. Merch by Amazon is ideal for selling custom t-shirt designs related to popular topics, products or memes. Commercial online print shops handle fulfillment after uploads. Trending searches and evaluating competitor shirt sales makes it easy to locate ideas ripe for strong conversions. Likewise, a platform like Teespring allows you to sell merchandise around niche fan groups from entertainment to politics and more both online and at live events.

Etsy Print Provider Partnerships

Etsy provides an immensely popular platform for crafters, artists, and specialty creatives to sell their wares—even if manufacturing is handled by partners. By setting up your Etsy shop, you can upload designs for items ranging from phone cases and notebooks to tapestries and mugs which integrated print providers produce on-demand once customers place orders. With both localized and global demand, Etsy allows creators to focus purely on design rather than operations.

Judicious Facebook & Instagram Marketing

The most effective way to drive continuous sales is targeted social media marketing campaigns — ideal for consistently testing print-on-demand and dropshipping income potential around different niche interests. With Facebook's detailed audience selectors, you can zero in on very specific product or design categories likely to convert based on interests and demographics. Instagram's shopping and product tagging features also make it easy to market niche items. Careful budgeting and result monitoring is critical for ensuring profitability however.

Dropshipping and print-on-demand platforms empower online sellers to experiment with physical product demand without endless effort or financial risk. Savvy research, marketing, automation, and analytics allow independent creators and entrepreneurs alike to leverage these immense ecommerce ecosystems. Testing niche products through Facebook ads, Etsy provider fulfillment, Merch by Amazon trend capitalization, and supplementary social media organic reach enable relatively hands-off income. With so many tools and services available today, generating passive sales around unique designs, specialty items, viral topics and niche fan bases is more accessible than ever. The only limit is your creative ideas and willingness to experiment.

CHAPTER FOUR

Build an Online Community

In the age of digital media and endless content, it's easier than ever to create materials that inform, educate, or entertain a target audience. Yet simply putting out quality content is not enough to truly engage that audience over the long term and turn them into loyal community members. True connection requires understanding people's deeper motivations and needs, solving their problems, and providing tangible value beyond informational materials alone. By taking a more holistic, service-centered approach, content creators can foster far more meaningful and lasting relationships.

Cater to Core Desires and Aspirations

Rather than taking a generic one-size-fits-all approach in your content and business, invest time upfront understanding why your audience consumes certain types of information and what emotional needs good content fulfills for them. For example, an outdoors enthusiast may follow camping content primarily for inspiration to support a lifestyle oriented around adventure and self-reliance. Really empathize with and speak to those core aspirations in all brand messaging — not just blog posts or videos.

Create Community Around Shared Lifestyle & Values

Content centered around a topic or hobby inherently appeals to those sharing common interests and values. Yet members also intrinsically yearn for community as part of their human need to belong. Thus, providing venues for your audience to interact allows them to support and learn from one another, not just consume your content as an isolated individual. Build online forums, host live meetups in local areas, develop insider clubs with access to community spaces, and foster opportunities for sharing knowledge.

Provide True Support and Problem-Solving

Rather than simply disseminating information, identify recurring questions your audience has that your content could answer or pain points it may ease. Show you truly understand their problems through personalized support avenues like exclusive email newsletters, direct message access channels, or member-only contact portals. Prioritize substantive responses to inquiries, perhaps connecting those struggling with others who've overcome similar hurdles thanks to your teachings. This humanizes your brand beyond being an aloof content source.

Collaborate on Product Recommendations

You likely suggest various products or services to assist readers with enacting the concepts from your content like guides for optimal camping gear or holistic self-care products. Yet there's opportunity to involve your audience more actively through collaborative recommendations showcasing items they personally validate. Solicit and feature product suggestions members have individually vetted and found valuable while tying their stories into the broader themes or values your brand centers on.

Motivate Through Success Stories

Speaking of storytelling, spinal-based narratives highlighting how both everyday community members and celebrated leaders living out your brand principles in inspirational ways motivate far more effectively thanisolated information alone. Put their compelling faces at the forefront. If you teach entrepreneurial concepts, profile small business owners who embody determined, empowered mindsets. Outdoorsy influencers can share adventurers overcoming epic challenges. These real-world examples vividly show your teachings manifested.

Mobilize Action through Challenges

True behavior change and the adoption of substantive lifestyle principles you teach require more than passive content absorption. Challenges actively motivate your audience into new habits and mindsets through fun community participation. Fitness influencers often leverage challenges centered on goal setting, tracking progress through shared spreadsheets, and motivating one another on social media groups toward real fitness accomplishments like races or benchmarks. This facilitates genuine connection through common effort.

Recognize Member Achievements

Speaking of goal crushing, spotlight user generated content from those hitting targets, completing challenges, or otherwise seeing tangible transformations from applying your teachings is incredibly validating while making members feel valued. Repost and praise challenge winners or members who hit milestone adoption of important principles like launching a successful small business. Feature their stories across social channels. Send direct gift boxes or rewards. This recognition for pan-community starsinvests everyone more deeply.

At the end of the day, people innately seek personal connections and community focused around mutual interests, shared mindsets, and common values. So meeting those relational needs through service offerings tailored to your distinctive audience supplements any content immensely when forging genuine bonds between brand and consumer. The solutions above help convert passive readers into enthusiastic community members truly aligned with your influencer brand vision.

Engaging Audiences Through Live Streaming

Live streaming represents an incredibly valuable opportunity to make deep connections with modern digital audiences. When done skillfully, streams foster community, allow two-way interaction, and provide value beyond passive consumption of stale content. Investing effort into hosting quality live sessions helps strengthen relationships and loyalty substantially. Use these proven techniques for maximizing engagement.

Plan Relevant, Dynamic Topics

Rather than just winging live sessions spontaneously, develop semi-structured plans mapping out core talking points related to current issues your audience cares about. Outline potential stories, unique takes, or novel solutions around challenges they regularly face. Have special guests lined up to bring fresh voices and domain expertise. Perhaps do an occasional "ask me anything" session. Schedule a calendar of themes centered on holidays, annual events related to your niche, or other temporal trends ripe for meaningful discussion.

Leverage Polls, Games and Contests

Interactive polls keep participants invested by allowing them to vote and shape direction in real time. For example, fitness hosts could poll fans on preferred target areas for a group challenge. Quizzes related to niche knowledge, pop culture or current events drive playful competition. Contest components like members submitting pet photos or best listener submissions judged on-air also facilitate lively community activity during the session rather than passivity.

Feature a Q&A Segment

Dedicate ten or fifteen minutes per stream for unstructured audience questions pulled from live chat or submissions. Not only does this provide helpful information to those listening later on but makes attendees feel valued by addressing their specific needs. Have moderators compile and screen questions ahead of time and provide them for review so responses sound natural versus caught off guard. Follow-ups post session via video or email show added care.

Incorporate Surprise Giveaways

The unexpected delights of surprise prizes or giveaways help spark excitement while also drawing in larger audiences seeking free merch, gift cards, or access to exclusive content. Distributing prizes randomly through the session keeps viewers tuned in and chatting. Require eligibility actions like sharing posts or retweeting helps expand reach virally. Just avoid making giveaways the main focus over delivering meaty value.

Go Behind the Scenes

Pulling back the curtain into your brand's inside operations intrigues audiences, strengthens perceived transparency, and humanizes you as more than just an icon personality. Give office tours, feature key team members, or showcase creative processes like songwriting techniques. Celebrity influencers could give glimpses into red carpet events or travel escapades. Outdoors hosts can highlight gear testing or planning recent adventures. These exclusive peeks make members feel special for tuning in live when reveals occur.

Collaborate with Special Guests

Inviting respected peers in your niche provides welcome alternate perspectives that enrich sessions considerably while expanding potential viewership by tapping into collaborators' fan bases simultaneously. The novelty factor also boosts attendance from the curious. Jointly interview an expert source. Have guests debate controversial niche issues. Collaborate on a group activity. Sessions become less predictable and more exciting while strengthening community bonds across creators and their combined followers when handled mutually beneficially.

Record and Repurpose Content

While live sessions provide unique value for attendees through direct access, recordings shared post session best leverage this rich content by allowing amplification potential to both existing and new audiences. Consider a special members only access window before public release. Chop edited highlight reels for social channels. Transcribe key excerpts into quote posts. Allow organic ongoing discovery through playlists. This magnifies the return on investment of quality streaming events.

By taking advantage of built-in tools for engagement, carefully structuring segmented content, and incorporating creative elements of surprise, exclusivity and access, influencers hosting live streams stand to boost audience interactivity and satisfaction immensely. Allocating additional effort for preparation, promotion, and repurposing ensures each event leverages maximum impact. Interactive streaming represents a hugely untapped opportunity for bonding with modern, digital first fans.

Fostering Connections Through Online Community

While high-quality content and digital courses provide value in their own right, today's audiences intrinsically crave community as well. Launching online spaces for discussion, intimate group coaching, and mastermind collaborations around shared interests or challenges meets relational needs while keeping users continually engaged with your brand. Build these community pillars thoughtfully, moderate actively, and nurture relationships authentically for maximum impact.

Craft Forums as Interactive Knowledge Bases

Online forums essentially function as searchable, ever-growing repositories of crowd-sourced answers to recurring questions or struggles your audience faces. Categorize forums around challenges

("Overcoming Launch Obstacles"), interests ("Favorite Launch Strategies), roles ("Site Developers Lounge") or product themes ("Theme Customizations"). Appoint moderators and seed initial discussions around hottest topics. Gently direct members to search before posting reduntancies. Welcome newbies warmly while relying on veteran users to shape culture.

Host Live Video Q&As and Panels

While traditional forums provide invaluable asynchronous support, real-time video Q&As bring conversations to life through interactive visibility and conversation. Host your own sessions or moderate vibrant panels featuring niche experts, celebrity influencers or enthusiastic power users. Collect questions beforehand through a shared doc or submissions to help guide discussion relevance. Manage the queue gently to allow organic interplay. Share replays along with rich notes recapping insights on the forums afterwards for amplification.

Spotlight User Success Stories

Leveraging forums to consistently highlight community members achieving breakthroughs or otherwise encapsulating your brand's principles in action provides inspiration for all while recognizing stellar participants. Allow members to nominate their peers' journeys. Ask standout users to document their stories natively as blog posts. With permission, re-share these spotlights across social media to spread motivation (and great UGC!). Send exclusive swag or access. This fosters upward mobility for all.

Offer Intimate Group Coaching

Small group coaching represents a profoundly impactful way to foster lasting transformation around life pursuits, health goals, artistic growth and more through intimate sharing, accountability and support. Define programs around outcomes centered on your teachings. Enrollment should feel exclusive. Place members into groups of 6 to 12 peers leading them through structured, multi-week curriculums concluding with celebratory graduation! Assign individual mentors for personalized guidance. Charge premium pricing given deep value.

Convene Insider Masterminds

Masterminds take group coaching a step further by convening 8 to 12 high-achieving individuals quarterly to collaborate intimately on business obstacles, share expertise and contacts, while providing mutual accountability and support. Given the investment of time, only accept members who meet well-defined success or growth benchmarks. maintain an application process. Host multi-day retreats to supplement video meetings allowing face time while planning action initiatives. Require NDAs given confidential nature.

Incentivize Valuable Contributions

Thoughtfully gamifying community participation builds intrinsic motivation through our innate drive for status and recognition. Establish a visible point system awarding badges and privileges for beneficial behaviors like posting insightful responses, contributing resources, welcoming new members, or referring friends. Perks may include profile badges, access to members-only content and events, discounts, free products, leader spotlights or prizes. Just ensure terms and privileges are clear upfront.

Launch Facebook Groups For Organic Interaction

Groups represent Facebook's own highly flexible forums variation with in-platform notification and discussion features integrateable into your website ecosystem. Take your niche community mobile through supplemental groups facilitating sharing advice, user generated content, informal live meetups powered by events features and chat. Appoint multiple moderators to model culture. Cross-promote new group launches through existing pages and profiles directing fans eager to connect into these new spheres.

While digital courses and content offer tremendous value, human beings innately seek community, relationships and belonging around shared interests and struggles. Launching online forums, intimate coaching cohorts and exclusive masterminds helps meet those profound emotional needs for members already resonating with your brand's purpose and principles. These community pillars boost engagement exponentially while providing venues for crowdsourced wisdom, accountability and celebration of success. Treat these spaces for connection as passion projects rather than sterile platforms. Nurture members with care and intention to help transform their lives holistically.

Building Bonds Through Chat

While delivering quality content certainly provides value for modern digital audiences, today's consumers intrinsically crave more meaningful connection as well. Thus integrating conversational interfaces like chat, messaging, and interactive comment features throughout your online platforms fosters greater engagement, loyalty, and satisfaction through relationship building.

Chat tools conveniently remove barriers to direct access while messaging apps enable ongoing dialogues, advice, and accountability between creators, influencers, coaches and their community members. Use these communication channels thoughtfully to strengthen bonds.

Incorporate Chatbots for Instant Assistance

AI-powered chatbots offer visitors and community members instantaneous support without requiring staff availability 24/7. Platforms like MobileMonkey and Chatfuel enable configuring conversational flows around common questions and struggles. Set up proactive triggers like delay responding to an email signup or abandoned shopping cart. Allow seamless handoff to human reps when needed.

Chatbots provide swift resolutions for simple inquiries like address changes, event details, refund policies or technical issues.

Members feel cared for through quick assistance while more complex matters route appropriately. Just ensure the experience remains intuitive.

Host Regular Video Office Hours

Designating set times for live streaming interactive video chat sessions makes you more accessible to community members through verbal and visual conversation. Publicize office hour schedules across your platform. Fans can ask niche questions, get coaching advice, share progress, or simply make meaningful connections.

Moderate the queue gently, allowing organic dialogue. Follow up privately afterwards if needed. Send brief video responses to unanswered questions. Save replays too!

Offer Direct Message Access

While chatbots and scheduled streams help, providing select super fans, coaching clients or premium members ways to directly message you drives meaningful rapport through personalized exchanges. Subscription sites like Mighty Networks enable configuring paid tiers granting direct messaging privileges with hosts and creators.

Be responsive but set expectations around any delays upfront. Follow message streams in batches as needed. This privileged access strengthens loyalty substantially even if conversations remain occasional.

Integrate Commenting Throughout

The ability to comment on blog posts, videos, podcast episodes, and really any content gives users a conduit for reactions, discussions and even building community around specific pieces of content. Email subscribers can even comment on newsletters driving further engagement.

Comments foster greater perceived relationship when creators actively participate in threads by tagging commenters gratitude or acknowledging their contributions. Hearting comments also increases return visits.

Facilitate Text Message Exchanges

For very intimate groups like high-level coaching cohorts or mastermind members, text messaging provides a familiar and trusted communications conduit. Platforms like Community allow organizing members into groups for ongoing text discussions, alerts and photo sharing. Schedule announcements are handy while chat archives prove helpful.

Naturally, provide members ways to opt out or mute conversations if volumes ever become excessive rather than intrusive. But used judiciously, text chat builds tight bonds.

In essence, digital community building requires a multifaceted communications approach today. While great content and courses provide the foundation, audiences equally value conversing directly with influencers and peers around niche topics of mutual interest through methods like chat, messaging, comments and text exchanges during their journey.

Enabling these streams of communication strengthens the creators-to-consumer relationship substantially over solely broadcasting content outward. Loyalty swells when fans feel a genuine rapport through back-and-forth dialogue with someone they respect. Meet this core need for interconnectivity using today's myriad technologies facilitators. Community expands exponentially when core human needs get fulfilled through belonging, mentorship and meaningful interactions.

CONCLUSION

The opportunities for generating income through online platforms are more abundant in today's digital landscape than ever before. And the best part is that virtually anyone with access to the internet can leverage their talents, skills, and creativity to carve out unique streams of revenue with minimal financial investment up front. Whether through freelancing services, monetizing creative works, dropshipping products, marketing affiliate links, building ecommerce stores, or launching digital content and communities tailored to underserved niches, ordinary individuals now possess tools previously only available to large corporations.

While certainly not without challenges, dedication and thoughtful strategy enable just about anyone to begin piecing together diverse income puzzles uniquely suited to their strengths and interests. And thanks to the global connectivity of internet marketing, potential audiences in the billions await any offer creatively addressing an emotional desire or solving a frustration they experience. The case studies and tactics covered throughout this book illustrate proven methodologies for tapping into several core income sources highly accessible in our digital moment.

But true success requires an entrepreneurial mindset centered on solving problems, adding value, and constantly learning rather than seeking mere quick wins. With patience and effective leverage of tools like social media, video, email marketing, affiliate promotions, advertising platforms, freelance job boards, print-on-demand services and ecommerce providers, you hold the power to build the lifestyle business of your dreams with relative autonomy. The only limits are those we place on ourselves. Creative solutions await for those bold enough to search for gaps and serve them well.

I sincerely hope you garnered insights and inspirations from this book that launch you on a journey toward greater fulfillment, prosperity and life on your own terms through generating income from digital opportunities all around you. Please connect online through my blog and social channels to provide feedback, share your own entrepreneurial journey, or simply support others chasing big dreams just like you.